TOM LATHAM

NEW ZEALAND CRICKETER

MR VIVEK KUMAR PANDEY

Contents

Foreword

Short Biography Of Tom Latham & Life Style, Career etc. During Writing This Book No Character, No Religion & No Caste Are Harmed. It's Only For Study Purpose. We don't want to hurt anyone.

Preface

Author biography in English :

MY NAME IS VIVEK KUMAR PANDEY . I WAS BORN IN 30 SEP 2002,I AM FROM SURAT GUJARAT INDIA.MY DREAM WAS TO BE GOOD WRITERS ,MY FAMILY SUPPORTED ME TO SUCCESSFUL AND I CAN DO IT MY SELF.How do I write? That is a question, I believe, that can be honestly answered by me."CELEBRATING YOUNGEST WRITER AWARD WINNER IN GUJARAT 1ST RANK" MR PANDEY JI . I may think I did a good job writing something. The reader is the one who decides the quality of my writing. I do find writing to be natural to me and therefore find it to be a real challenge. My trick as a challenged writer is to do the best I can and know that I am happy with the final outcome. It may take a while to do my best and there may be quite a few problems I run into along the way.

I am not a greedy person those who are thinking about me and my self I never tried it anyone people suffering from sadness ,I trying to get promoted people suffering from happiness and joy in your Life Time. Now in current situation in India and also world people are unemployed and have no many but our indian governor help to people to get free food from ration card , i also take part in leadership team ,i am Motivational speaker , Film script writer. There was my two dream firstly writer and secondly actor & also my own film is upcoming soon i done almost completely completed script for my film .I AM GOING TO SAY WORD OF HEART TOUCH OUT PLEASE READ IT" , firstly i thanks my father he supports me in this field they always getting inspired me by own his words and behavior ,they always said that he was a biggest person in the world in future and also they purchase fruit and chocolate for me in anytime & anyway , firstly my father buy him then call me Vivek you want a chocolate i will say yes papa but how many tell me ,papa: you tell me how much i buy him i told 1 or 2 chocolate but my father purchase whole the boxes of chocolate and they get suprised me. MY FATHER WAS BORN IN " 20 SEPTEMBER" 1971 IN INDIA.

1) MY FATHER FAVORITE CLOTHES IS KURTA PAIJMA AND ALSO STYLES SHOE

2) FAVORITE SINGER IS KISHORE DA

3) FAVORITE STATE GUJARAT AND KOLKATA , HIS VILLAGE IN BIHAR

4) FAVORITE COLOR BLACK AND WHITE

THEY ALSO LOVE cricket like IPL and one day t-20 .they also like watching a News daily and heard the song daily ,they also interested in tik tok video but in current time tik tok is banned in india but also few videos are in you tube. In lockdown time my family and me very enjoy day daily. my father play daily ludo with his sister and son, daughter.they always loved tea and coffee anytime call me . I make it tea for my father but some reason after the April to june they are suffering from fever and cough , weakness on 6 June 2020 my father death. they not told me say bye bye his life. After death of 6 June on 10 june my mom and dad anniversary.but my father is Best in the world they can do anything for me please take care of father and respect it of your parents.

Tom Latham

- **Tom Latham**

1. Short Biography Of Tom Latham & Life Style, Career etc. During Writing This Book No Character, No Religion & No Caste Are Harmed. It's Only For Study Purpose. We don't want to hurt anyone.

Thomas William Maxwell Latham (born 2 April 1992) is a New Zealand international cricketer who is vice-captain of the New Zealand cricket team in Tests and ODIs. He is the son of former cricketer Rod Latham.He is primarily a batsman who also plays as a wicket-keeper. Playing for Canterbury, he made his first-class cricket debut against Central Districts in 2010 in the Plunket Shield. He was selected for the One-Day International series against Zimbabwe in 2012 and made his ODI debut on 3 February 2012. He made his Test match debut against India in February 2014.

- **Tom Latham Domestic cricket career**

Latham made his debut for Canterbury in the 2010–11 Plunket Shield season, scoring 65 in his maiden first-class cricket innings. He had played youth cricket for Canterbury, captaining the under-19 side, and played for the Canterbury A team from the 2008–09 season. During 2010 Latham had been a member of the Durham County Cricket Club academy in England. He played matches for Durham Second XI and a Northumberland development XI as well as playing club cricket in the North East Premier League in England for Gateshead Fell.

Latham has appeared in all formats of the game for Canterbury. He spent the 2013 English summer playing in north-east England again, playing for South Shields in the North East Premier League and Scotland in the 2013 Yorkshire Bank 40 competition, the major English List A competition in 2013, as well as making two further appearances for Durham's second XI. He was selected for the touring New Zealand Test squad during the summer and for the T20 squad, playing in both T20 internationals on the tour.

Kent signed Latham as an overseas player for the 2016 English season. He made his County Championship debut against Glamorgan at Canterbury in May, scoring half-centuries in both innings, the first Kent batsman in history to do so on debut. After playing in all three formats of the game for the county, Latham left Kent in mid-July to join the New Zealand team in Zimbabwe.In 2017 Latham signed as an overseas player with Durham for the second half of the 2017 English cricket season.

- **Tom Latham International career**

Latham scored 24 runs on debut, batting at number five, in an ODI against Zimbabwe in 2012. He made his Twenty20 International debut against the West Indies on 30 July, making 15 and 19 in the series. Latham also played in the tour's ODI series but failed to contribute significantly, his highest score being 32. He was recalled against Bangladesh, where he played a bright innings of 43 while opening the batting, and scored a match-winning 86 off 68 balls during the following tour of Sri Lanka.

He made his Test match debut against India in February 2014, with scores of 29 and 0. He then toured the West Indies with New Zealand in June, playing in all three Tests and two T20s. He had a highly successful Test series, scoring three half-centuries and 288 runs in total, finishing second in the series list of top run scorers, just behind teammate Kane Williamson. In doing so he helped his side to an overseas series victory. By July 2014 he had claimed the spot of opener after a run of poor form for incumbents Hamish Rutherford and Peter Fulton. His first Test century was achieved against Pakistan in Abu Dhabi, on 11 November 2014; he scored 103.

Despite his position as an opening batsman in Test matches, Latham was named as a middle-order batsman and backup wicket-keeper to Luke Ronchi for the 2015 Cricket World Cup. He also shared Test wicket-keeping duties against England with BJ Watling, keeping for New Zealand in the first Test at Lord's following an injury to Watling. When he is not a keeper he generally fields close to the wicket or in the slips.

Latham was selected to tour Zimbabwe in 2015 as an opening batsman. During the second ODI of the series, he scored his maiden ODI century of 110 not out as part of an unbeaten partnership with Martin Guptill of 236 as

New Zealand won the match by 10 wickets to level the series. In the third Test against Australia in the 2015-16 Trans–Tasman Trophy, the first ever day-night Test match, Latham became the first man to score a fifty in a day-night Test.In October 2016, while playing against India at Dharamshala Latham became the tenth batsman and the first New Zealander to carry his bat in an ODI.

In January 2017 Latham was named as the New Zealand wicket-keeper for the Chappell-Hadlee series. In the first ODI of that series he equalled New Zealand's record of five dismissals as a wicket keeper in an ODI innings. Due to poor form with the bat,however, he was dropped on 1 March for the series against South Africa.

In May 2017 Latham was recalled and named as captain for the Ireland Tri-Series against Ireland and Bangladesh in Ireland with a number of regular players playing in the 2017 Indian Premier League.In October 2017, Latham was given the wicketkeeping duties against India and moved down to no. 5 due to his ability to play against spin. He scored 103* from 102 balls in game 1 of the 3-match series.In December 2017 Latham resumed his role as acting ODI captain against West Indies with Kane Williamson and Tim Southee rested.

In May 2018, he was one of twenty players to be awarded a new contract for the 2018–19 season by New Zealand Cricket. In December 2018, against Sri Lanka, he made the highest score while carrying the bat in Test cricket, with 264 not out. In April 2019, he was named in New Zealand's squad for the 2019 Cricket World Cup. In July 2019, in New Zealand's semi-final match against India, Latham played in his 150th international match for New Zealand.In January 2020, in the third Test against Australia, Latham captained New Zealand for the first time in Test cricket, after Kane Williamson was ruled out of the match due to flu.In February 2020, in the first and second ODI against India, Latham captained New Zealand to win by 4 Wickets and 22 runs after Kane Williamson was ruled out of the match due to a shoulder injury.

- **Tom Latham List of international centuries**

Latham has scored 12 centuries in Test cricket and six in One Day Internationals matches. His highest Test score of 264 not out came against Sri Lanka at the Basin Reserve in December 2018 and his highest ODI score of 140 not out was made against the Netherlands at Seddon Park in Hamilton in April 2022.

CHAPTER TWO

New Zealand national cricket team

- **New Zealand national cricket team**

The New Zealand national cricket team represents New Zealand in men's international cricket. Named the Black Caps, they played their first Test in 1930 against England in Christchurch, becoming the fifth country to play Test cricket. From 1930 New Zealand had to wait until 1956, more than 26 years, for its first Test victory, against the West Indies at Eden Park in Auckland. They played their first ODI in the 1972–73 season against Pakistan in Christchurch.

The current captain in all formats of the game is Kane Williamson, who replaced Brendon McCullum after the latter's retirement in December 2015. The national team is organised by New Zealand Cricket.

The New Zealand cricket team became known as the Blackcaps in January 1998, after its sponsor at the time, Clear Communications, held a competition to choose a name for the team. This is one of many national team nicknames related to the All Blacks.

- As of 19th November 2021, New Zealand have played 1383 international matches, winning 539, losing 618, tying 15 and drawing 167 matches while 44 matches ended as no result. The team is ranked 1st in Tests, 1st in ODIs and 3rd in T20Is by the ICC. New Zealand have reached two World Cup finals, in 2015 and 2019. They defeated South Africa in the semi final of the 2015 World Cup, which was their first win in the a world cup semi final, but they ultimately lost to Trans-Tasman rivals Australia. In the next World Cup in 2019, New Zealand again reached the final which they lost to the hosts England on boundary count after the match and the subsequent Super Over both ended as ties.

The 2000 ICC KnockOut Trophy win (now referred to as ICC Champions Trophy) stands as one of two ICC tournaments won by the team in their cricketing history. New Zealand also won the inaugural ICC World Test Championship tournament in 2021, beating India by 8 wickets.

- **Beginnings of cricket in New Zealand**

The reverend Henry Williams provided history with the first report of a game of cricket in New Zealand, when he wrote in his diary in December 1832 about boys in and around Paihia on Horotutu Beach playing cricket. In 1835, Charles Darwin and HMS Beagle called into the Bay of Islands on its epic circumnavigation of the Earth and Darwin witnessed a game of cricket played by freed Māori slaves and the son of a missionary at Waimate North. Darwin in The Voyage of the Beagle wrote.

several young men redeemed by the missionaires from slavery were employed on the farm. In the evening I saw a party of them at cricket.

The first recorded game of cricket in New Zealand took place in Wellington in December 1842. The Wellington Spectator reports a game on 28 December 1842 played by a "Red" team and a "Blue" team from the Wellington Club. The first fully recorded match was reported by the Examiner in Nelson between the Surveyors and Nelson in March 1844.

The first team to tour New Zealand was Parr's all England XI in 1863–64. Between 1864 and 1914, 22 foreign teams toured New Zealand. England sent 6 teams, Australia 15 and one from Fiji.

- **First national team**

On 15–17 February 1894 the first team representing New Zealand played New South Wales at Lancaster Park in Christchurch. New South Wales won by 160 runs. New South Wales returned again in 1895–96 and New Zealand won the solitary game by 142 runs, its first victory. The New Zealand Cricket Council was formed towards the end of 1894.

New Zealand played its first two internationals (not Tests) in 1904–05 against a star-studded Australia team containing such players as Victor Trumper, Warwick Armstrong and Clem Hill. Rain saved New Zealand from a thrashing in the first match, but not the second, which New Zealand lost by an innings and 358 runs – currently the second largest defeat in New Zealand first-class history.

- **Inter-war period**

In 1927 NZ toured England. They played 26 first-class matches, mostly against county sides. They won seven matches, including those against Worcestershire, Glamorgan, Somerset and Derbyshire. On the strength of the performances of this tour New Zealand was granted Test status.

In 1929/30 the M.C.C toured NZ and played 4 Tests all of 3 days in duration. New Zealand lost its first Test match but drew the next 3. In the second Test Stewie Dempster and Jackie Mills put on 276 for the first wicket. This is still the highest partnership for New Zealand against England. New Zealand first played South Africa in 1931–32 in a three match series but were unable to secure Test matches against any teams other than England before World War II ended all Test cricket for 7 years. A Test tour by Australia, planned for February and March 1940, was cancelled after the outbreak of the war.

- **After World War II**

New Zealand's first Test after the war was against Australia in 1945/46. This game was not considered a "Test" at the time but it was granted Test status retrospectively by the International Cricket Council in March 1948. The New Zealand players who appeared in this match probably did not appreciate this move by the ICC as New Zealand were dismissed for 42 and 54. The New Zealand Cricket Council's unwillingness to pay Australian players a decent allowance to tour New Zealand ensured that this was the only Test Australia played against New Zealand between 1929 and 1972.

In 1949 New Zealand sent one of its best ever sides to England. It contained Bert Sutcliffe, Martin Donnelly,

John R. Reid and Jack Cowie. However, 3-day Test matches ensured that all 4 Tests were drawn. Many have regarded the 1949 tour of England among New Zealand's best ever touring performances. All four tests were high-scoring despite being draws and Martin Donnelly's 206 at Lord's hailed as one of the finest innings ever seen there. Despite being winless, New Zealand did not lose a test either. Prior to this, only the legendary 1948 Australian team, led by the great Don Bradman, had achieved this.

New Zealand played its first matches against the West Indies in 1951–52, and Pakistan and India in 1955/56.

In 1954/55 New Zealand recorded the lowest ever innings total, 26 against England. The following season New Zealand achieved its first Test victory. The first 3 Tests of a 4 Test series were won easily by the West Indies but New Zealand won the fourth to notch up its first Test victory. It had taken them 45 matches and 26 years to attain.

- **New Zealand vs West Indies**

255 all out (166.5 overs)
John R. Reid 84
Tom Dewdney 5/21 (19.5 overs)
145 all out (78.3 overs)
Hammond Furlonge 64
Harry Cave 4/22 (27.3 overs)
157 all out (80 overs)
Sammy Guillen 41
Denis Atkinson 7/53 (40 overs)
77 all out (45.1 overs)
Everton Weekes 31
Harry Cave 4/21 (13.1 overs)

New Zealand won by 190 runs
Eden Park, Auckland
Umpires: Clyde Harris (NZL) and Terry Pearce (NZL)

- **New Zealand won the toss and chose to bat**

In the next 20 years New Zealand won only seven more Tests. For most of this period New Zealand lacked a class bowler to lead their attack although they had two excellent batsmen in Bert Sutcliffe and Glenn Turner and a great all-rounder in John R. Reid.

Reid captained New Zealand on a tour to South Africa in 1961–62 where the five test series was drawn 2–2. The victories in the third and fifth tests were the first overseas victories New Zealand achieved. Reid scored 1,915 runs in the tour, setting a record for the most runs scored by a touring batsman of South Africa as a result.

New Zealand won their first test series in their three match 1969/70 tour of Pakistan 1–0.This was the first ever series win by New Zealand after almost 40 years and 30 consecutive winless series.

- **1970 to 2000**

Scoreboard - Basin ReserveFebruary 1978. NZ's first win over England

In 1973 Richard Hadlee debuted and the rate at which New Zealand won Tests picked up dramatically. Hadlee was one of the best pace bowlers of his generation, playing 86 Tests for New Zealand, before he retired in 1990. Of the 86 Tests that Hadlee played in New Zealand won 22 and lost 28. In 1977/78 New Zealand won its first Test against England, at the 48th attempt. Hadlee took 10 wickets in the match.

During the 1980s New Zealand also had the services of one of its best ever batsman, Martin Crowe and a number of good players such as John Wright, Bruce Edgar, John F. Reid, Andrew Jones, Geoff Howarth, Jeremy Coney, Ian Smith, John Bracewell, Lance Cairns, Stephen Boock, and Ewen Chatfield, who were capable of playing the occasional match winning performance and consistently making a valuable contribution to a Test match.

The best example of New Zealand's two star players (R. Hadlee and M. Crowe) putting in match winning performances and other players making good contributions is New Zealand versus Australia, 1985 at Brisbane. In Australia's first innings Hadlee took 9–52. In New Zealand's only turn at bat, M Crowe scored 188 and John F. Reid 108. Edgar, Wright, Coney, Jeff Crowe, V. Brown, and Hadlee scored between 17 and 54*. In Australia's second innings, Hadlee took 6–71 and Chatfield 3–75. New Zealand won by an innings and 41 runs.

8–12 November 1985
Scorecard

- **Australia vs New Zealand**

179 (76.4 overs)
Kepler Wessels 70 (186)
Richard Hadlee 9/52 (23.4 overs)
553/7d (161 overs)
Martin Crowe 188 (328)
Greg Matthews 3/110 (31 overs)
333 (116.5 overs
Allan Border 152* (301)
Richard Hadlee 6/71 (28.5 overs)

New Zealand won by an innings and 41 runs
The Gabba, Brisbane
Umpires: Tony Crafter (Aus) and Dick French (Aus)
Player of the match: Richard Hadlee (NZ)

- **New Zealand won the toss and elected to field.**

One-day cricket also gave New Zealand a chance to compete more regularly than Test cricket with the better sides in world cricket. In one-day cricket a batsman does not need to score centuries to win games for his side and bowlers do not need to bowl the opposition out. One-day games can be won by one batsman getting a 50, a few others getting 30s, bowlers bowling economically and everyone fielding well. These were requirements New Zealand players could consistently meet and thus developed a good one-day record against all sides.

Perhaps New Zealand's most infamous one-day match was the "under arm" match against Australia at the MCG in 1981. Requiring six runs to tie the match off the final ball, Australian captain Greg Chappell instructed his brother Trevor to "bowl" the ball underarm along the wicket to prevent New Zealand batsman Brian McKechnie from hitting a six. The Australian umpires ruled the move as legal even though to this day many believe it was one of the most unsporting decisions made in cricket.

When New Zealand next played in the tri-series in Australia in 1983, Lance Cairns became a cult hero for his one-day batting. In one match against Australia, he hit six sixes at the MCG, one of the world's largest grounds. Few fans remember that New Zealand lost this game by 149 runs. However, Lance's greatest contribution to New Zealand cricket was his son Chris Cairns.

Chris Cairns made his debut one year before Hadlee retired in 1990. Cairns, one of New Zealand's best all-rounders, led the 1990s bowling attack with Danny Morrison. Stephen Fleming, New Zealand's most prolific scorer, led the batting and the team into the 21st century. Nathan Astle and Craig McMillan also scored plenty of runs for New Zealand, but both retired earlier than expected.

Daniel Vettori made his debut as an 18-year-old in 1997, and when he took over from Fleming as captain in 2007 he was regarded as the best spinning all-rounder in world cricket. On 26 August 2009, Daniel Vettori became the eighth player and second left-arm bowler (after Chaminda Vaas) in history to take 300 wickets and score 3000 test runs, joining the illustrious club. Vettori decided to take an indefinite break from international short form cricket in 2011 but continued to represent New Zealand in Test cricket and returned for the 2015 Cricket World Cup.

On 4 April 1996, New Zealand achieved a unique world record, where the whole team was adjudged Man of the Match for team performance against 4 run victory over the West Indies. This is recorded as the only time where whole team achieved such an award.

- **The Black Caps logo.**

New Zealand started the new millennium by winning the 2000 ICC KnockOut Trophy in Kenya to claim their first ICC tournament. They started with a 64-run win over Zimbabwe then proceeded to beat Pakistan by 4 wickets in the semi-final. In the final against India, Chris Cairns scored an unbeaten 102 in New Zealand's run chase helping them win the tournament.

- **New Zealand won the 2000 ICC Knockout Trophy.**

Shane Bond played 17 Tests for NZ between 2001 and 2007 but missed far more through injury. When fit, he added a dimension to the NZ bowling attack that had been missing since Hadlee retired.

- **The New Zealand team celebrating a dismissal in 2009**

The rise of the financial power of the BCCI had an immense effect on NZ cricket and its players. The BCCI managed to convince other boards not to pick players who had joined the rival Twenty-20 Indian Cricket League. NZ Cricket lost the services of Shane Bond, Lou Vincent, Andre Adams, Hamish Marshall and Daryl Tuffey. The money to be made from Twenty-20 cricket in India may have also induced players, such as Craig McMillan and Scott Styris (from Test cricket) to retire earlier than they would have otherwise. After the demise of the Indian Cricket League Bond and Tuffey again played for New Zealand.

Vettori stood down as Test captain in 2011 leading to star batsman Ross Taylor to take his place. Taylor led New Zealand for a year which included a thrilling win in a low scoring Test match against Australia in Hobart, their first win over Australia since 1993. In 2012/13 Brendon McCullum became captain and new players such as Kane Williamson, Corey Anderson, Doug Bracewell, Trent Boult and Jimmy Neesham emerged as world-class performers. McCullum captained New Zealand to series wins against the West Indies and India in 2013/14 and both Pakistan and Sri Lanka in 2014/15 increasing New Zealand's rankings in both Test and ODI formats. In the series against India McCullum scored 302 at Wellington to become New

Zealand's first Test triple centurion.

1. In early 2015 New Zealand made the final of the Cricket World Cup, going through the tournament undefeated until the final, where they lost to Australia by seven wickets.
2. In 2015 the New Zealand national cricket team played under the name of Aotearoa for their first match against Zimbabwe to celebrate te Wiki o te Reo Māori (Māori Language Week).
3. In mid-2015 New Zealand toured England, performing well, drawing the Test series 1–1, and losing the One Day series, 2–3.
4. From October to November 2015, and in February 2016, New Zealand played Australia in two Test Series, in three and two games a piece
5. With a changing of an era in the Australian team, New Zealand was rated as a chance of winning especially in New Zealand. New Zealand lost both series by 2-0

History of cricket

- **History of cricket**

The sport of cricket has a known history beginning in the late 16th century. Having originated in south-east England, it became an established sport in the country in the 18th century and developed globally in the 19th and 20th centuries. International matches have been played since the 19th-century and formal Test cricket matches are considered to date from 1877. Cricket is the world's second most popular spectator sport after association football (soccer).

Internationally, cricket is governed by the International Cricket Council (ICC) which has over one hundred countries and territories in membership although only twelve currently play Test cricket.

- **Origin**

Cricket was probably created during Saxon or Norman times by children living in the Weald, an area of dense woodlands and clearings in south-east England that lies across Kent and Sussex. The first definite written reference is from the end of the 16th-century.

There have been several speculations about the game's origins, including some that it was created in France or Flanders. The earliest of these speculative references is from 1300 and concerns the future King Edward II playing at "creag and other games" in both Westminster and Newenden. It has been suggested that "creag" was an Old English word for cricket, but expert opinion is that it was an early spelling of "craic", meaning "fun and games in general".

It is generally believed that cricket survived as a children's game for many generations before it was increasingly taken up by adults around the beginning of the 17th century. Possibly cricket was derived from bowls, assuming bowls is the older sport, by the intervention of a batsman trying to stop the ball from reaching its target by hitting it away. Playing on sheep-grazed land or in clearings, the original implements may have been a matted lump of sheep's wool (or even a stone or a small lump of wood) as the ball; a stick or a crook or another farm tool as the bat; and a stool or a tree stump or a gate (e.g., a wicket gate) as the wicket.

- **First definite reference**

John Derrick was a pupil at the Royal Grammar School, then the Free School, in Guildford when he and his friends played creckett circa 1550.

In 1597 (Old Style – 1598 New Style) a court case in England concerning an ownership dispute over a plot of common land in Guildford, Surrey, mentions the game of creckett. A 59-year-old coroner, John Derrick, testified that he and his school friends had played creckett on the site fifty years earlier when they attended the Free School. Derrick's account proves beyond reasonable doubt that the game was being played in Surrey circa 1550, and is the earliest universally accepted reference to the game.

The first reference to cricket being played as an adult sport was in 1611, when two men in Sussex were prosecuted for playing cricket on Sunday instead of going to church. In the same year, a dictionary defined cricket as a boys' game, and this suggests that adult participation was a recent development.

- **Derivation of the name of "cricket"**

A number of words are thought to be possible sources for the term "cricket". In the earliest definite reference, it was spelled creckett. The name may have been derived from the Middle Dutch krick(-e), meaning a stick; or the Old English cricc or cryce meaning a crutch or staff, or the French word criquet meaning a wooden post. The Middle Dutch word krickstoel means a long low stool used for kneeling in church; this resembled the long low wicket with two stumps used in early cricket. According to Heiner Gillmeister, a European language expert of the University of Bonn, "cricket" derives from the Middle Dutch phrase for hockey, met de (krik ket)sen (i.e., "with the stick chase").

It is more likely that the terminology of cricket was based on words in use in south-east England at the time and, given trade connections with the County of Flanders, especially in the 15th century when it belonged to the Duchy of Burgundy, many Middle Dutch words found their way into southern English dialects.

- **The Commonwealth**

After the Civil War ended in 1648, the new Puritan government clamped down on "unlawful assemblies", in particular the more raucous sports such as football. Their laws also demanded a stricter observance of the Sabbath than there had been previously. As the Sabbath was the only free time available to the lower classes, cricket's popularity may have waned during the Commonwealth. However, it did flourish in public fee-paying schools such as Winchester and St Paul's. There is no actual evidence that Oliver Cromwell's regime banned cricket specifically and there are references to it during the interregnum that suggest it was acceptable to the authorities provided that it did not cause any "breach of the Sabbath". It is believed that the nobility in general adopted cricket at this time through involvement in village games.

- **Gambling and press coverage**

Cricket thrived after the Restoration in 1660 and is believed to have first attracted gamblers making large bets at this time. It is possible, as believed by some historians, that top-class matches began. In 1664, the "Cavalier" Parliament passed the Gaming Act 1664 which limited stakes to £100, although that was still a fortune at the time, equivalent to about £16,000 in present-day terms. Cricket had become a significant gambling sport by the end of the 17th century, as evidenced in 1697 by a newspaper report of a "great match" played in Sussex which was 11-a-side and played for high stakes of 50 guineas a side.

With freedom of the press having been granted in 1696, cricket for the first time could be reported in the newspapers. But it was a long time before the newspaper industry adapted sufficiently to provide frequent, let alone comprehensive, coverage of the game. During the first half of the 18th century, press reports tended to focus on the betting rather than on the play.

- **18th-century cricket**

Gambling introduced the first patrons because some of the gamblers decided to strengthen their bets by forming their own teams and it is believed the first "county teams" were formed in the aftermath of the Restoration in 1660, especially as members of the nobility were employing "local experts" from village cricket as the earliest professionals. The first known game in which the teams use county names is in 1709 but there can be little doubt that these sort of fixtures were being arranged long before that. The match in 1697 was probably Sussex versus another county.

The most notable of the early patrons were a group of aristocrats and businessmen who were active from about 1725, which is the time that press coverage became more regular, perhaps as a result of the patrons' influence. These men included the 2nd Duke of Richmond, Sir William Gage, Alan Brodrick and Edwin Stead. For the first time, the press mentions individual players like Thomas Waymark.

- **Cricket expands beyond England**

Cricket was introduced to North America via the English colonies in the 17th century, probably before it had even reached the north of England. In the 18th century it arrived in other parts of the globe. It was introduced to the West Indies by colonists and to India by East India Company mariners in the first half of the century. It arrived in Australia almost as soon as colonisation began in 1788. New Zealand and South Africa followed in the early years of the 19th century.

Cricket never caught on in Canada, despite efforts by the upper class to promote the game as a way of identifying with the "mother country". Canada, unlike Australia and the West Indies, witnessed a continual decline in the popularity of the game during 1860 to 1960. Linked in the public consciousness to an upper-class sport, the game never became popular with the general public. In the summer season it had to compete with baseball. During the First World War, Canadian units stationed in France played baseball instead of cricket.

- **Development Laws of Cricket**

It's not clear when the basic rules of cricket such as bat and ball, the wicket, pitch dimensions, overs, how out, etc. were originally formulated. In 1728, the Duke of Richmond and Alan Brodick drew up Articles of Agreement to determine the code of practice in a particular game and this became a common feature, especially around payment of stake money and distributing the winnings given the importance of gambling.

In 1744, the Laws of Cricket were codified for the first time and then amended in 1774, when innovations such as lbw, middle stump and maximum bat width were added. These laws stated that "the principals shall choose from amongst the gentlemen present two umpires who shall absolutely decide all disputes". The codes were drawn up by the so-called "Star and Garter Club" whose members ultimately founded the Marylebone Cricket Club at Lord's in 1787. The MCC immediately became the custodian of the Laws and has made periodic revisions and recodifications subsequently.

- **Continued growth in England**

The game continued to spread throughout England, and, in 1751, Yorkshire is first mentioned as a venue. The original form of bowling (i.e., rolling the ball along the ground as in bowls) was superseded sometime after 1760 when bowlers began to pitch the ball and study variations in line, length and pace. Scorecards began to be kept on a regular basis from 1772; since then, an increasingly clear picture has emerged of the sport's development.

- **An artwork depicting the history of the cricket bat**

The first famous clubs were London and Dartford in the early 18th century. London played its matches on the Artillery Ground, which still exists. Others followed, particularly Slindon in Sussex, which was backed by the Duke of Richmond and featured the star player Richard Newland. There were other prominent clubs at Maidenhead, Hornchurch, Maidstone, Sevenoaks, Bromley, Addington, Hadlow and Chertsey.

But far and away the most famous of the early clubs was Hambledon in Hampshire. It started as a parish organisation that first achieved prominence in 1756. The club itself was founded in the 1760s and was well patronised to the extent that it was the focal point of the game for about thirty years until the formation of MCC and the opening of Lord's Cricket Ground in 1787. Hambledon produced several outstanding players including the master batsman John Small and the first great fast bowler Thomas

Brett. Their most notable opponent was the Chertsey and Surrey bowler Edward "Lumpy" Stevens, who is believed to have been the main proponent of the flighted delivery.

It was in answer to the flighted, or pitched, delivery that the straight bat was introduced. The old "hockey stick"–style of bat was only really effective against the ball being trundled or skimmed along the ground. First-class cricket began, retrospectively, in 1772.A Game of Cricket at The Royal Academy Club in Marylebone Fields, now Regent's Park, depiction by unknown artist, c. 1790–1799

- **History of cricket (1772–1815) and History of English cricket (1816–1863)**

The game also underwent a fundamental change of organisation with the formation for the first time of county clubs. All the modern county clubs, starting with Sussex in 1839, were founded during the 19th century. No sooner had the first county clubs established themselves than they faced what amounted to "player action" as William Clarke created the travelling All-England Eleven in 1846. Though a commercial venture, this team did much to popularise the game in districts which had never previously been visited by high-class cricketers. Other similar teams were created and this vogue lasted for about thirty years. But the counties and MCC prevailed.

- **A cricket match at Darnall, Sheffield in the 1820s.**

The growth of cricket in the mid and late 19th century was assisted by the development of the railway network. For the first time, teams from a long distance apart could play one other without a prohibitively time-consuming journey. Spectators could travel longer distances to matches, increasing the size of crowds. Army units around the Empire had time on their hands, and encouraged the locals so they could have some entertaining competition. Most of the Empire embraced cricket, with the exception of Canada.

In 1864, another bowling revolution resulted in the legalisation of overarm and in the same year. W. G. Grace began his long and influential career at this time, his feats doing much to increase cricket's popularity. He introduced technical innovations which revolutionised the game, particularly in batting.

- **International cricket begins**

The first ever international cricket game was between the US and Canada in 1844. The match was played at the grounds of the St George's Cricket Club in New York.

- **The English team 1859 on their way to the US**

In 1859, a team of leading English professionals set off to North America on the first-ever overseas tour and, in 1862, the first English team toured Australia. Between May and October 1868, a team of Aboriginal Australians toured England in what was the first Australian cricket team to travel overseas.

- **The first Australian touring team (1878) pictured at Niagara Falls**

In 1877, an England touring team in Australia played two matches against full Australian XIs that are now regarded as the inaugural Test matches. The following year, the Australians toured England for the first time and the success of this tour ensured a popular demand for similar ventures in future. No Tests were played in 1878 but more soon followed and, at The Oval in 1882, the Australian victory in a tense finish gave rise to The Ashes.South Africa became the third Test nation in 1889.

- **National championships**

A significant development in domestic cricket occurred in 1890 when the official County Championship was constituted in England. Soon afterwards, in May 1894, the sport's first-class standard was officially defined. This organisational initiative has been repeated in other countries. Australia established the Sheffield Shield in 1892–93. Other national competitions to be established were the Currie Cup in South Africa, the Plunket Shield in New Zealand and the Ranji Trophy in India. The ICC re-defined first-class status in 1947 as a global concept.

The period from 1890 to the outbreak of the First World War has become one of nostalgia, ostensibly because the teams played cricket according to "the spirit of the game", but more realistically because it was a peacetime period that was shattered by the First World War. The era has been called The Golden Age of cricket and it featured numerous great names such as Grace, Wilfred Rhodes, C. B. Fry, Ranjitsinhji and Victor Trumper.

- **Balls per over**

During most of the 19th-century standard overs were made up of four deliveries. In 1889 five-ball overs were introduced in first-class cricket, with a move to generally use six-ball overs in 1900.

In the 20th-century, eight-ball overs were used at times in a number of countries, primarily Australia, where eight-balls were the standard over length between 1918/19 and 1978/79, South Africa and New Zealand. Since the 1979/80 Australian and New Zealand seasons, six balls per over have been used worldwide, and the most recent version of the Laws only permits six-ball overs.

- **Growth of international cricket**

Sid Barnes traps Lala Amarnath lbw in the first official Test between Australia and India at the MCG in 1948

The Imperial Cricket Conference was founded in 1909 with England, Australia and South Africa as the founder members. This aimed to regulate international cricket between the three sides, considered the only three of equal status at the time. West Indies were admitted as members in 1928, allowing them to play Test cricket against the other sides. New Zealand and India both became Test playing nations before World War II and Pakistan joined soon afterwards in 1952.

At the initial suggestion of Pakistan, the ICC was expanded to include non-Test playing countries from 1965, with Associate members being admitted. At the same time the organisation changed its name to the International Cricket Conference. The first limited-overs World Cups were played during the 1970s and Sri Lanka became the first Associate member to be raised to Test playing status in 1982.

The international game continued to grow with the introduction of Affiliate Member status in 1984, a level of membership designed for sides with less history of playing cricket. In 1989 the ICC renamed itself the International Cricket Council. Zimbabwe became Full Members in 1992 and Bangladesh in 2000 before Afghanistan and Ireland were both admitted as Test sides in 2018, bringing the number of full members of the ICC to 12.

- **International cricket in South Africa from 1971 to 1981**

The greatest crisis to hit international cricket was brought about by apartheid, the South African policy of racial segregation. The situation began to crystallise after 1961 when South Africa left the Commonwealth of Nations and so, under the rules of the day, its cricket board had to leave the International Cricket Conference (ICC). Cricket's opposition to apartheid intensified in 1968 with the cancellation of England's tour to South Africa by the South African authorities, due to the inclusion in the England team of Basil D'Oliveira, a Cape Coloured player. In 1970, the ICC members voted to suspend South Africa indefinitely from international cricket competition.

Starved of top-level competition for its best players, the South African Cricket Board began funding so-called "rebel tours", offering large sums of money for international players to form teams and tour South Africa. The ICC's response was to blacklist any rebel players who agreed to tour South Africa, banning them from officially sanctioned international cricket. As players were poorly remunerated during the 1970s, several accepted the offer to tour South Africa, particularly players getting towards the end of their careers for which a blacklisting would have little effect.

The rebel tours continued into the 1980s but then progress was made in South African politics and it became clear that apartheid was ending. South Africa, now a "Rainbow Nation" under Nelson Mandela, was welcomed back into international sport in 1991.

- **World Series Cricket**

The money problems of top cricketers were also the root cause of another cricketing crisis that arose in 1977 when the Australian media magnate Kerry Packer fell out with the Australian Cricket Board over TV rights. Taking advantage of the low remuneration paid to players, Packer retaliated by signing several of the best players in the world to a privately run cricket league outside the structure of international cricket. World Series Cricket hired some of the banned South African players and allowed them to show off their skills in an international arena against other world-class players. The schism lasted only until 1979 and the "rebel" players were allowed back into established international cricket, though many found that their national teams had moved on without them. Long-term results of World Series Cricket have included the introduction of significantly higher player salaries and innovations such as coloured kit and night games.

- **Limited-overs cricket**

In the 1960s, English county teams began playing a version of cricket with games of only one innings each and a maximum number of overs per innings. Starting in 1963 as a knockout competition only, limited-overs cricket grew in popularity and, in 1969, a national league was created which consequently caused a reduction in the number of matches in the County Championship. The status of limited overs matches is governed by the official List A categorisation. Although many "traditional" cricket fans objected to the shorter form of the game, limited-overs cricket did have the advantage of delivering a result to spectators within a single day; it did improve cricket's appeal to younger or busier people; and it did prove commercially successful.

The first limited-overs international match took place at Melbourne Cricket Ground in 1971 as a time-filler after a Test match had been abandoned because of heavy rain on the opening days. It was tried simply as an experiment and to give the players some exercise, but turned out to be immensely popular. limited-overs internationals (LOIs or ODIs—one-day internationals) have since grown to become a massively popular form of the game, especially for busy people who want to be able to see a whole match. The International Cricket Council reacted to this development by organising the first Cricket World Cup in England in 1975, with all the Test-playing nations taking part.

- **Analytic and graphic technology**

Limited-overs cricket increased television ratings for cricket coverage. Innovative techniques introduced in coverage of limited-over matches were soon adopted for Test coverage. The innovations included presentation of in-depth statistics and graphical analysis, placing miniature cameras in the stumps, multiple usage of cameras to provide shots from several locations around the ground, high-speed photography and computer graphics technology enabling television viewers to study the course of a delivery and help them understand an umpire's decision.

In 1992, the use of a third umpire to adjudicate run-out appeals with television replays was introduced in the Test series between South Africa and India. The third umpire's duties have subsequently expanded to include decisions on other aspects of play such as stumpings, catches and boundaries. From 2011, the third umpire was being called upon to moderate review of umpires' decisions, including lbw, with the aid of virtual-reality tracking technologies (e.g., Hawk-Eye and Hot Spot), though such measures still could not free some disputed decisions from heated controversy.

- **21ˢᵗ-century cricket**

In June 2001, the ICC introduced a "Test Championship Table" and, in October 2002, a "One-day International Championship Table". As indicated by ICC rankings, the various cricket formats have continued to be a major competitive sport in most former British Empire countries, notably the Indian subcontinent, and new participants including the Netherlands. In 2017, the number of countries with full ICC membership was increased to twelve by the addition of Afghanistan and Ireland.

The ICC expanded its development programme, aiming to produce more national teams capable of competing at the various formats. Development efforts are focused on African and Asian nations, and on the United States. In 2004, the ICC Intercontinental Cup brought first-class cricket to 12 nations, mostly for the first time. Cricket's newest innovation is Twenty20, essentially an evening entertainment. It has so far enjoyed enormous popularity and has attracted large attendances at matches as well as good TV audience ratings. The inaugural ICC Twenty20 World Cup tournament was held in 2007. The formation of Twenty20 leagues in India – the unofficial Indian Cricket League, which started in 2007, and the official Indian Premier League, starting in 2008 – raised much speculation in the cricketing press about their effect on the future of cricket.